ENDORSEMENTS

I am in awe of the courage my friend Donna Beaver has to write a book with such transparency. And she includes pictures of her journey as well. Donna has written her testimony in her book, *Through Storms, Struggles and Fire*, and illustrates the power of God's redeeming work even when we face life's greatest challenges. This book needs to be read by your friends and family and you. Don't miss out. This is a great life story.

Alice Smith
U.S. Prayer Center
Houston, TX
http://www.usprayercenter.org

Through Storms, Struggles and Fire, is the story of one woman's triumphant journey and adventure through some very challenging times.

Donna Beaver is a dedicated follower of Jesus Christ and if you haven't had the pleasure of meeting her or knowing her like I do, then you'll find that it won't take very long for you to discover the intimate and authentic "love" relationship that she shares with her Lord and her Redeemer, Jesus Christ. If you presently find yourself facing a severe *storm*, or perhaps you might be in a present *struggle* of your own, or maybe the temperature of life has risen lately, because you've entered a "fiery" trial—then I suggest, that you do yourself a favor and find a quiet place somewhere and decide to walk through the pages of Donna's journey. I assure you, by the time you cross her finish line with her, you will have received strength, insights and much encouragement for the journey that awaits you.

> Pastor Philip Cappuccio
> *Kingdom Life Covenant Church*
> Hershey, PA

Donna is an incredible Christian! She is a passionate witness for Christ and her love for Him is simply contagious. She can't stop talking about the Lord who radically changed her life. At our first encounter I adopted her as my mother in the Lord and we are knitted in the Spirit to spread the message of the Kingdom of God. Our relationship is a divine connection and God has made her a mentor to me and multitudes.

When she imparts truth, immediately, hope is presented and faith is offered to catch the best opportunities of heaven. Our Lord is real to Donna and she believes everybody needs to meet and know her best friend, Jesus. Her story is captivating and as you read this book you will find an authentic twenty-first century believer engaged with a mission to announce to anyone who will listen about His amazing love and power to heal. This book will create a fusion of faith to hold fast and not give up.

Donna has gone through a journey of faith that will make you cry, shout and tell everyone about the power of God that is at work for His creation.

Pastor Eddie Cross
Senior Leader
Miracle Life Church
Harrisburg, PA

A day, a week, a year, a century...How much time is needed to know the length, and breadth, and width, and height of the love God has for each life?

My friend, Donna Beaver, is a carrier of this truth.

May the truth she shares in this book spill over onto you in ways only God can design.

For His Glory,
Mary Krueger
Modesto, CA

"I have been in ministry for almost 30 years (all at the same church) and without a doubt, Donna is one of the most godliest women I know! She has a deep love for Jesus and a great understanding of the power of prayer in the life of a follower of Christ. She has been a huge blessing in my personal life and the life of many others! I highly recommend her book."

Rick Countryman
Senior Pastor
Big Valley Grace Community Church
Modesto, CA

Through
STORMS
STRUGGLES
and
FIRE

Text design and typesetting by Webbdezyne.
Cover design by Karen Webb.
www.webbdezyne.com

Hudson Photography
Oakdale, California
Photo on author page by Marian Miller.
www.nhudsonphoto.com

ISBN: 978-1-482323-31-3

For Worldwide Distribution, Printed in the U.S.A.

1 2 3 4 5 6 7 / 17 16 15 14 13

Through
STORMS
STRUGGLES
—*and*—
FIRE

ONE WOMAN'S TESTIMONY *of*
the GREATNESS *of* GOD
IN *the* MIDST *of* CHALLENGING TIMES

DONNA BEAVER

Love & Blessings,

Danna Beaver

Jeremiah 33:3

Beaver girls and family left to right: Paul and Johanna, Katie and Zachary Alves (in front). Then Joey, Heather, Heidi and Joshua Thomas in the back row and Mom (NaNa) in the middle. Front row: Lindsay, Mom – Luanne, Brianna, Ashley and Husband Steve.

DEDICATION

I dedicate this book to my daughters, my sons-in-law, and my precious grandchildren. I pray this book will be a revelation of the goodness of the Lord—not only in my life, but in their lives too.

ACKNOWLEDGMENTS

First of all I want to give glory to my Lord and Savior Jesus Christ.

I also give thanks to my pastor, my family and friends, and my intercessors whose prayers have brought me through this time and to the place where I am today.

I thank my doctors: Dr. Dente, Dr. Kostin, and Dr. Liu for the way they walked beside me while I was in their care.

I also say a special thank you to Alice Smith for the words of encouragement she gave me as I began writing my book—the words that blessed my heart, "Donna, I am so proud of you."

CONTENTS

FOREWORD

"I have known Donna Beaver for the past 25 years. I have come to appreciate her in so many ways. She's an amazingly authentic person (as you will discover in the pages of this book). She lives her life "wide open." New ventures don't scare her. The varied opinions of others don't intimidate her. Difficult situations don't diminish her faith. And difficult people don't decrease her capacity to love.

She's not "Superwoman." She's a very real woman. And her transparency continues to bring hope and healing to so many of us.

There is no deep secret to the way Donna lives her life. Simply put, she "lives loved." She knows who her Father is. She knows what He thinks about her. And she lives like she is His favorite daughter, because she receives His love and His promises just that way.

I have watched Donna walk through some of life's most difficult experiences. Losses. Disappointments. Set-backs. And betrayals.

Her resilience has not come from sheer determination—a steely resolve to "tough it out." In fact, she has never been one to act "tough."

It's her tenderness that has sustained her. For she has found the place of tender trust in the goodness of God to be the safest place of all. She has refused to be hardened by hard circumstances, or overwhelmed by overwhelming odds.

She's discovered "the place" Jesus promised to prepare for us. A place to live life from. A place He described simply as: "Where I am, there you may also be."

As you read Donna's story, I invite you to discover that place too. It's a resting place. An anchor for your soul.

And once you go there... you'll never want to leave!"

So there you go.

So proud of you...and grateful for you!

Much love,

Dave Hess
Senior Pastor
Christ Community Church
Camp Hill, Pennsylvania
Author of *Hope Beyond Reason*

INTRODUCTION

What I am about to share with you is the story of my journey through several storms that passed through my life during the years 2010 and 2011. You may be familiar with the one storm's name—cancer—and the terror, pain, and heartache it can leave behind. Cancer is a name like Katrina (the deadly hurricane that devastated the Florida Gulf Coast in 2005)—just mentioning it conjurers up thoughts of death and destruction. Well, the name of the storm in my journey has a lower case "c" because Christ is the big "C." Christ is the One who took me through *the storm, the struggles, and the fire.*

My hope is that in reading my story you will become aware of how much Jesus Christ loves you, protects you, watches over you, and holds you in His arms. No matter what satan may throw at you—in the end, what he had planned for destruction was turned around so that when you stepped out of the fire, you don't even smell like smoke and you're not burned. After any storm, struggle, or fire, you will have an amazing testimony of how great and awesome God really is.

While sharing my personal thoughts along with excerpts from my diary and emails to friends who were praying for me, I share how God has brought me through some of the most challenging times of my life. In the midst of these storms I received: words of knowledge from complete strangers; visions of angels; expedited healing; prayers from friends; the love and service of many; and most of all, I knew that Jesus Christ was standing beside me!

I pray you are encouraged in your walk with Jesus by reading this book; and if you don't know Him, that you come into a personal relationship with Him by inviting Him into your heart this very moment— you will never be the same!

May these words be a soothing balm to your soul, and may Jehovah Rapha (The Lord who Heals) bring His healing touch to whatever part of you that is broken and full restoration and renewed hope to whatever storm or struggle you are going *through* in your life.

Forever be blessed by His great love,

Donna Beaver

I

ABUNDANT LIVING IN THE MIDST OF THE STORM

The thief does not come except to steal, and to kill, and to destroy. I [Jesus] have come that they may have life, and that they may have it more abundantly (John 10:10).

I have felt the need in my heart to share what God has done for me over the past two years. Looking back, I believe things were set in motion in the spiritual realm when I came into a position of leadership concerning prayer for the State of Pennsylvania in January 2010. Living in Pennsylvania, I knew the importance of its place in history and how America had been founded as a godly nation, so I joined with many others to intercede for my state. I was soon to realize the importance of having a prayer covering for myself while carrying Christ's banner into battle. I believe that we need to cry out more to the Lord today to restore our country. We need fearless warriors who do not fear what the enemy may throw at them—warriors whose eyes are on an eternal gain and the victory we have already won.

The Attack and Recovery

It was Monday, March 1, 2010, and life was wonderful. It was a beautiful spring day, my business was flourishing, and I was thanking the Lord for all His goodness as I drove to an afternoon meeting. Afterward, I decided to stop and visit my daughter. Again counting my blessings thinking, *To have children who know Jesus and walk with Him...*

I stepped out of the car and remember seeing my son-in-law standing on the porch—we both said "Hello" to one another. And that's when it hit me. Now if I asked my doctor, she would say, "Donna, you're no spring chicken. You just had a bad fall... your foot slipped." If you ask me—the one living in this body—I'd say something threw me to the ground with such force that I thought every bone in my body was broken.

I was slammed onto the cement curb hitting my right knee, then the right side of my face smashed into the cement foundation of my daughter's house (I had my glasses on), my ring on my right hand scraped along the cement, and my head hit so hard that my right earring flew off. The first thought that came to my mind after I caught my breath was, *Wow, God! What was that about?* I watched through a haze as my son-in-law ran down the stairs, picked me up, and helped me into the house.

After my son-in-law laid me on the couch, I immediately asked for my cell phone. The very next thought I had was to call a close friend of mine. I dialed her number, and when she answered I simply said, "Pray for me, I've smashed my eye" and hung up. Then I called my friend Mary from Christ Community Church and said something similar, "Pray for me, I've smashed my face." (The amazing thing about this is how little you need to say to an intercessor at the time of an emergency for them to know what to do.) After those two phone calls, I prayed out loud, "Jesus take the trauma away." I prayed that sentence three times. It may sound strange, but later I would realize the importance of those words.

As soon as I had finished praying, my daughter Heidi, a registered nurse, came through the door from working at the local hospital. With her husband's help, they immediately loaded me into the car and drove me to the hospital. While there, I had a CT scan of my face, head, and neck, and x-rays of my right knee. My face was bruised and my right eye was swollen shut. My right knee cap was out of place because of the swelling so they sent me home with a leg brace. And through it all I was praising God, "No broken bones! Thank You, Jesus!"

I got home late that Monday night and stayed in the house for the next two weeks healing my bumps and bruises with soaking prayer and worship. *How abundant are His blessings, how wonderful are His ways—* these thoughts permeated my mind, heart, and spirit.

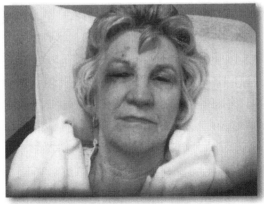

Donna Beaver, March 1, 2010

Diary Entry: March 7, 2010

My heart cry today is to stand in His righteousness. Having the truth of His word and speaking only words that encourage and edify others. Knowing and speaking, "Greater is He who is in me than he who is in the world." As I wake this morning lying in bed, I write the words that He has given me, "Seek Me first, pray for those in leadership—for those who are on the front line, come together to cover each other in My precious blood and My mighty protection."

All I have walked through—much stuff—I'm reminded that even in the midst of physical or emotional pain we must give Him our praise. Praise Him for He is Holy! Holy! Holy! He loves us and has a plan for everything that we go through—if we can just trust Him and release everything to Him. Even when we don't understand why—He is there and will never leave us.

The funny thing that I remember about this past week—I remember I was praising the Lord because I didn't want to say that "I was under attack." I did not want to receive that— it was very hard because that was the week that Frank (my husband) had passed away. Also, all my grandbabies called because my picture went out to everybody. And so I heard from all of them, "Nana, what happened to you!" and of course my daughters, too. It was a tough week, even after nine years I'm grieving—yet I wanted to praise the Lord so much last week because I knew He protected me. It certainly was a time of trusting and resting in His peace.

Thank You, Lord, for those who You have sent to be with me in my time of recovery— helping hands and hearts filled with love and understanding and especially those who have prayed for me. How generous are Your benefits!

The Importance of Prayer

Through the fall and the subsequent recovery, the Lord showed me the importance of prayer for each other, coming together for a prayer covering.

Be anxious for nothing, but in everything by prayer and supplication, with thanksgiving, let your requests be made known to God (Philippians 4:6).

It was several years ago that the Lord laid upon my heart the outline of The Circle of Prayer to draw us even closer to Jesus. He wants us to grow closer in our time of prayer with Him. Husbands, wives, friends, pastors, mentors, all coming together in the name of Jesus to pray for each other is one of the most important things we can do as the body of Christ. The coming together for prayer with three or more people is found in Ecclesiastes 4:12, *"Though one may be overpowered by another, two can withstand him. And a threefold cord is not quickly broken."*

I can't encourage Christians enough to pray for each other—sharing with one another what the Lord is saying to you. We need to join together for our leaders, our pastors, their wives, our ministries, and certainly our family and friends. Remember to always pray for those on the front lines!

The Importance of "Those" Words

Remember reading earlier when I prayed, "Jesus take the trauma away!"? Why would I say "trauma"? "Jesus take the *trauma* away!" I said that three times instead of, "Jesus be with me," or "Jesus help me." Trauma was speaking against the attack that satan had just done to me. I realized later that trauma is when we go through something violent—and what could be more violent than satan attacking me as he did. As time went on and people spoke to me and prayed with me, I realized more and more what an outright attack it was. Later I would hear powerful words from a prophet who had never met me before but spoke specifically about what satan had done to me and how God protected me—I write about this in an upcoming chapter.

The Miracle of the Glasses

After two weeks, I was well enough to leave the house and drive my car. I thought, *What a miracle to be healed up enough to venture out in such a short time from such a traumatic experience!* That morning I had a prayer meeting to attend and then another appointment with my orthopedic doctor. But before I left the house, I decided to look for my glasses (the ones I had been wearing when my head hit the cement foundation). I looked everywhere, but couldn't find them. I called my daughter Heidi and asked if she remembered seeing them. She said, "Joey put them in my glass case and left them in your car." As I got ready to leave, I found the case in my car and opened it to look at my glasses. They were badly scratched. I put them away and thought about what to do with them while on my way to the prayer meeting.

After the prayer meeting, I decided to stop at the eye doctor before my next appointment to see if they could buff the scratches off the lens or possibly replace it if it was too damaged. When I walked into the office, I told the young man what had happened to my glasses—how I had fallen and damaged them. He opened the case and looked at them to assess the damage, then asked me to wait while he took them into another room to work on them. It was only moments later that he reappeared and handed them back to me. I looked at the glasses and asked, "How did you do that so quickly?" They looked brand-new. He said, "There was heavy oil on the glass that protected the lens." I knew immediately what it was.

As I left the eye doctor's office, I began praising the Lord and laughing joyfully. "Lord, You had my angel put heavy oil on my lens to protect my eye!" I began to realize that my guardian angel was there in the midst of a great attack—where bones could have been broken and my eye severely damaged— God had all things in His hands! "What an awesome God You are!" I said out loud as I walked to my car, "Especially at a time when the enemy was looking to wipe me out…You were there!"

*For He shall give His angels charge over you,
to keep you in all your ways* (Psalm 91:11).

The thing I've come to realize is that God has plans for our lives and a unique destiny for each of us—and our angels are with us to help fulfill His plan and purpose! It's wonderful when you suddenly realize that God sent an angel into your life because He loves you, because He knew you in your mother's womb.

For You formed my inward parts; You covered me in my mother's womb (Psalm 139:13).

Looking back, I am amazed at the abundance of blessings through this whole experience and how close Jesus has been throughout my life. The same is true for you. My heart cry for you is to keep your eyes on Him—especially during the times we live in. He is our strength and protection in every situation we face.

2

CALLED TO A
HIGHER PURPOSE

*For I know the thoughts that I think
toward you, says the LORD, thoughts of
peace and not of evil, to give you a fu-
ture and a hope* (Jeremiah 29:11).

It was the second week after my assault when
a dear friend came to visit and encourage me. But
before I talk about our visit that day, I have to go
back in time to the month of September in 2009.
That month I had been in California. I had gone
to a prayer ministry there and had bought all the
materials on prayer and intercession. When I was

on the plane coming home, I heard the Lord speak to me, "You're to go to the Susquehanna River—to the head or the beginning of the river." I was like, "Okay, Lord." I received it, but didn't think about it. On my return, I had heard that many people had prayed over the Susquehanna River, so I decided to lay the thought down. I shrugged my shoulders and thought, *I guess I don't need to do that.*

Well the months flew by as I was in prayer for our State, to March 1, the day of my attack—and now to where my friend sat before me bringing me flowers to brighten my day. As we talked, she suddenly looked at me and said, "Donna, are you prophetic?" and I thought, *Probably a little prophetic at times.* And I said, "Why...why do you ask me that?" She said, "Well, I believe you are to go to the head of the Susquehanna River, where it begins." And so I said, "Okay." I thought, *Father, forgive me that I didn't listen to You before.*

A Prayer Mission

So it was the words, "Are you prophetic?" that set me on a wonderful journey with three others on March 26, 2010. Fortified spiritually with the full realization of the Lord's protection, I felt fully ready for the prayer mission God was sending me on. I asked Mary, Nancy, and Bob to go with me. Bob is anointed in praying for lost souls. Bob called me and said he didn't think he was to go. My response was, "Okay," thinking, three was perfect for the journey. The Lord laid everything out for me, concerning what we were to do. We were to anoint each other with oil, we were to take communion, and pray over each other. He also said we were to take salt (for the salt covenant),[1] and oil to the river, wine and bread, and we were to take the staff or rod to pray into the river. We were to declare the glory of the Lord over the Susquehanna River. And so we did this.

The day before our trip to find the head of the river, Bob contacted me and felt led by the Lord to go with us. So the four of us went to Cooperstown, New York, and then drove around to see how it was going to work out. I'm driving at this time even with a bum leg. When we reached Lake Otsego, we got out and walked around to find out where the head of the river actually was. We spotted three young women standing by the lake talking to each other. I walked over and asked, "Do you know where the actual beginning of the Susquehanna is?" They said, "Oh yes, just drive up there and you'll see the road." So we drove up the road, and there was no place to park. That whole side of the area was loaded with cars. I said, "Let's just pray—the Lord has this lined up for us—so let's pray!"

While we were all quietly praying, Bob said, "We could park downtown and walk back." I said, "Maybe you can, but I can't...I've got a bum knee!" and laughed. As we drove around again, it was amazing to see not a car in sight. The cars were all gone—nobody was there! So we parked the car and opened the trunk. We anointed each other with oil, took communion together, prayed, and then we took the other elements down to the river.

Donna Beaver with staff a the head of the Susquehanna.

There before us was the very beginning of the Susquehanna River. We began praying and then carried out the Salt Covenant. We poured the bread and wine into the water and prayed over that, then I stood with the staff by the river and declared that this river was mighty for the Lord and that all the evil that had come through this river would be gone. Nancy rolled up her pant legs—even though it was 32 degrees and freezing—as she felt led by the Lord to go into the river. I said, "Okay, go for it, but take the rod with you." So she walked out into the river praising the Lord—and fell in! I yelled, "Get yourself out...I'm not coming in after you!" We all laughed, but my heart was heavy for her because it was really cold. She picked up the rod and walked back to shore. Now, we have a girl who is all wet. We put her in the back seat and helped her take off her wet clothes. We covered her with a blanket, and I gave her my jacket. We decided to go downtown to get coffee to warm up and find some clothes for her for the ride home.

Miracle of Seven Eagles

After drinking our coffee and getting back into the car, Bob said, "Donna, I forgot to put this marker in the ground with the Scripture on it where we were standing." So I said, "Okay, Bob, whatever you need to do, we'll just sit in the car while you do it." We drove back to where we were by the lake, and Bob got out of the car and started walking down the hill to put his stake into the ground. As I was sitting in the car, I felt the Lord wanted me to get out. I said to the women, "You know what, I feel like I need to get out of the car." I got out and looked up at the sky. There was an eagle…one, two, three, four, five, and six, then seven eagles! Seven eagles were circling over the area where we had been. They were soaring over us. I began to cry as I heard the Lord say He was pleased with what I had done—what He had asked me to do. I got back into the car crying and told the women, "God is so pleased with what we've done!" We were so thankful that we went back! What an adventure with the Lord, and I knew there was more to come.

> *But those who wait on the LORD shall renew their strength; they shall mount up with wings like eagles, they shall run and not be weary, they shall walk and not faint* (Isaiah 40:31).

Another Assault, Another Victory

After the trauma of my fall, I ended up with psoriasis on my head, ears, and neck. I was a mess. They say that trauma brings on psoriasis—so I knew where it came from and continued to stay strong in the Lord about it, rebuking it, and not accepting it upon my body. From the end of March and into April and May, I had to deal with this awful condition, but this did not deter my prayer ministry. Next we were going to Three Mile Island. Three other women came with me and we prayed for the Susquehanna River across from Three Mile Island—this was in August 2010. After this I went to California, and then my hair started falling out from the psoriasis. September, October, and November I started wearing little hats to cover my thinning hair.

But the very hairs of your head are all numbered (Matthew 10:30).

Then I started putting on a natural hair replacement product that my company sells. While doing this, I praised the Lord and would pray, "Lord give me a bushy, full head of hair!" I continued to praise Him and thank Him for bringing my hair back. And in January 2011, my hair was back and the psoriasis gone. Maybe I don't have the bush look, but my hair was back and looking great. God is so wonderful.

The Doctor's Appointment

In late November 2010, I had my annual doctor's appointment with Doctor Dente. She is like one of my daughters; we always find time to talk and have fun conversations because I always feel great. But this time she asked, "Donna, is anything going on?" I thought back to a car accident I had seven years previous—I associated the pain I had in the left side of my rib cage with that. So my reply was, "Well...I have a pain in my left rib cage—it's from that car accident I was in seven years ago when I cracked my ribs." She said, "Let's order a CT scan and see what it's all about."

So this was the next step in my journey.

ENDNOTE

1. Mat. 5:30, Lev. 2:13. YHWH's Salt Covenant (Hebrew, b'rith melah), is the most extraordinary of all HIS Covenants....Traditionallly salt was shared to seal a truce....Salt Purifies. http://www.homeworship101.com/fyi_salt_covenant.htm (accessed 12/25/12).

3

Into the Fire

...the fire had no power; the hair of their head was not singed nor were their garments affected, and the smell of fire was not on them (Daniel 3:27).

It was right after Christmas 2010 and I was at my daughter Luanne's home who lives in New York State. While I was there, Doctor Dente called and left a message that something was showing on the scan and she wanted to do a second one. When I called her back, she said, "We need to do a second scan right away." I had the second scan as she recommended because I was leaving for Florida on January 15th for 4 to 5 weeks.

Not long after this—the Wednesday before I was to leave—I received a call from my doctor saying I needed to have a biopsy done on my right lung.

The news that I needed a lung biopsy sure didn't sound good to me and I really had a hard time making the decision to do it. It was even more difficult asking anyone to pray for me. I didn't call any of my prayer partners or friends. I didn't want to call anyone, because I didn't want to face the fact that I might have cancer. I had been a pray partner at the local hospital and had been praying with cancer patients for several years. I remembered what I had always said to them— "Cancer is the small 'c' and Christ is the big 'C.'" Now I stood in their shoes, hearing the echo of the words I spoke over them coming back to minister to me.

As I prayed that Wednesday night, I cried. I kept asking the Lord, "Who should I call or what should I do?" I didn't want to tell anyone that I had cancer. I was devastated.

The Miracle Email

It was around 10 P.M. that evening when I received an email from Alice Smith. I had met Alice about ten years previous, a few months after my husband, Frank, died. Alice has a mighty intercessory ministry called the *U.S. Prayer Center*. She and her husband, Eddie, are from Houston, Texas, and they have books and resources regarding intimacy with Jesus, intercession, deliverance, and spiritual warfare.[1] I had been asked by my church's Women's Ministry if I would host her while she was speaking at our church. I knew I was to do that, so with no reservation, I said, "Yes I would love to host Alice and her traveling partner." This meant that I would pick them up from the hotel and bring them back and forth to Christ Community Church.

As she ministered, I received such a revelation in the words she spoke and saw things in a new light. She taught on body, soul, and spirit. When we sang an old hymn together—"It is Well with My Soul"—I remembered that we sang the same song at Frank's funeral, but it didn't feel right in my soul. As we sang the familiar words of the chorus, I realized it may not be "well with my *soul*," but it was well with my *spirit,* because I knew Frank was with the Lord.

We are confident, yes, well pleased rather to be absent from the body and to be present with the Lord (2 Corinthians 5:8).

The connection we shared while I was with Alice was very profound. A number of years passed, and in 2008 I went to be part of her prayer team at a local convention center (there is a prayer team praying behind the scenes—which Alice leads—while ministry is going on). Two years had passed since then, so I had not heard from Alice in all this time.

Now, sitting at my computer at 10 o'clock at night and seeing the email from her suddenly pop up made my jaw drop open. Then, just as suddenly, the Lord said to me, "Send her an email and ask her to pray for you." So I did. I wrote, "Alice would you pray for me?" Then I got up and got ready for bed. It was 10:30 when I went to turn off the computer and there was an email from Alice, "Donna, give me your phone number and I'll call you in the morning."

In the morning she called me and said, "Donna, tell me what's been going on." So I told her about being involved with prayer ministry for Pennsylvania. And how on March 1st the enemy shoved me and I hurt my right knee and right eye. And then I said, "OH! My right lung!" and it hit me. That it was the right side of my body that was being attacked—the authority of Jesus! And that's what she spoke. She said, "Satan is trying to take the authority of Jesus out of your life." It is the right hand, the right side of our bodies that symbolize the authority of Christ.

I've never had anybody pray like she prayed over me then. "Donna, in the name of Jesus I come against the attack of satan on the authority of Jesus Christ in your life!" Then she said, "Donna, go to Florida. Enjoy yourself. Have joy and praise the Lord!" That was Wednesday, and on Saturday I knew I would be leaving for Florida. I have two daughters who are nurses and they were saying, "Mom, what are you doing?" To which I replied, "I'm going to Florida, I'm going to praise the Lord! I'm going to take off!" And I did.

A Word from a Stranger

After my return from Florida, I sent an email to Alice:

Hi, Alice.

I just wanted to catch you up on what's been going on. I arrived home on Friday from Florida. Thank you for praying and encouraging me to take this trip—God is so faithful! On my way flying down, I sat next to this older gentleman. I was sharing about how wonderful Jesus is. Because we were in the exit row I told him, "Well I could change seats with you because you might

need to help me lift this door if there's an emer-
gency—but don't worry, Jesus is in charge and
we'll be fine." That's what opened our conver-
sation and got us laughing.

I never said anything about what I was walking
through medically—not talking about myself—
just sharing Jesus. He was a very nice Catholic
man, and his wife was flying in another row. His
son and daughter-in-law were in first class be-
cause she flew for Delta airlines. As he talked,
he looked at me and said, "You will have a long
life because the Lord has much for you to do."
Then he said to me, "You are His messenger."
It blew me away. I had to get up and run to the
bathroom to praise the Lord, "God, You are
so awesome that You would have this man—a
complete stranger who doesn't know anything
about what I'm going through—speak a word
over my life right from Your heart to encour-
age me! Thank You, Lord, for giving me ears
to hear your words of destiny spoken to me!"

It was Monday, January 17, 2011, my first
week in Florida. I looked up at the clock after
waking up that morning and it showed 3:33. I
asked the Lord, "What are You saying to me?"
I always question the Lord—what are You say-
ing to me, what do You want me to do, or what

are You showing me in that? I went to the bath-room and then couldn't sleep so I turned on the television. Of all people, there was a women preacher from Jacksonville, Florida saying, **"Call to me, and I will answer you, and show you great and mighty things, which you do not know"** *(Jeremiah 33:3). (I just saw that num-ber on the clock!)*

Lord, what could be a great and mighty thing that I can't even imagine but with You I can! *Then I heard her say Psalm 118:8-9,* **"It is bet-ter to trust in the Lord than to put confidence in man. It is better to trust in the Lord than to put confidence in princes."** *I thought,* **Okay Lord, I'm going to put my trust in You.** *Then I read down to Psalm 118:15-16,* **"The voice of rejoicing and salvation is in the tents of the righteous...."**

Now listen to this, "The right hand of the Lord does valiantly, the right hand of the Lord is ex-alted, the right hand of the Lord does valiantly, I shall not die, but live, and declare the glory of the Lord." The words "right hand" I said three times and three times they are written in the word. I will share later what the Lord gave to me in my Circle of Prayer, then you'll know why the number 3 is so important to me.

Tomorrow morning I go for my biopsy at the local medical center. I'm going to trust in my wonderful Lord for the plans that He has for me for the rest of my days.

Alice, I bless your ministry and thank you for your wonderful prayer over me.

Love and blessings,

Donna

I was resting in His peace knowing: *I shall not die, but live, and declare the glory of the Lord. You have long life because the Lord has much for you to do. You are His messenger.* These thoughts wrapped around me and permeated my heart and spirit as I prepared to ride out the storm of cancer with Jesus by my side.

ENDNOTE

1. For more information about the Alice and Eddie Smith's ministry, visit: www.usprayercenter.org.

4

STANDING FIRM ON
HIS PROMISES

I shall not die, but live, and declare the
works of the LORD (Psalm 118:17).

I enjoyed my trip to Florida and came home
with a renewed strength. I went for my biopsy the
first Wednesday after my return. Everything went
smoothly and with little discomfort. I continued
my life as usual—not wanting to sit around moping
or worrying about what the results would be. My
friend Melanie picked me up Friday morning and

we made plans to have lunch after praying for the people at the hospital.

At the hospital in the prayer room that day, I had the opportunity to pray with two women in wheel chairs with oxygen attached to their noses. They both had lung cancer. The enemy seemed to be roaring at me that day, "This is your fate!" But I remembered God's promises in my heart and spirit standing firm, not only for myself but for these dear people too.

Receiving the News

When we left the hospital there was a message from Doctor Dente on my cell phone. Melanie asked, "Aren't you going to listen to it?" I answered her by saying not until after we have lunch. I thought I had better eat first before hearing whatever my doctor had to say. Enjoying the last few moments with a friend before hearing what could be weighty news. Again while we were eating lunch Melanie asked, "Are you sure you want to wait until after lunch?" "Yes," I said.

She brought me home and came into the house with me. When we got into my house I listened to the message. I heard Doctor Dente say, "Donna call me, you have a cancer spot on your right lung." Then she said, "Donna, we'll get through this."

It's hard to say how you feel or what you are thinking when you hear the news that you have cancer. I would like to tell you I stood strong—yes I still held the word of God in my heart—but physically and emotionally I fell apart. This was not what I wanted to do, but it is what happened.

After gathering myself together, I first called my pastor, Dave Hess. I've attended Christ Community Church in Camp Hill, Pennsylvania, for twenty-eight years. Pastor Dave is a wonderful man of God who has also walked through cancer and has written a book about his experience titled *Hope Beyond Reason*. It was wonderful to have him pray for me, and I knew God was with me. It was after Pastor Dave's prayer that I knew I must call my daughters. I called Johanna, then Heidi, but Luanne was out of town, so I decided to tell her later. Melanie, who had stayed by my side through all the phone calls, had to leave, but said she would come back later.

When Doctor Dente called back, she asked me if she could line up all that needed to be done and I said, "You know I trust you, so schedule whatever procedures I need." She called back in twenty minutes and had all my appointments scheduled. She had worked for Doctor Kostin years before, and he was going to be my surgeon. I was pleased that everything had been set up but began to feel over-whelmed as I stretched out on my couch. Then my friend Melanie, who is a breast cancer survivor, came through the door and said, "Donna, we are going to beat this battle!" She prayed mighty words over me. How wonderful to have a friend who knows the fire ahead and stands with you in prayer.

Again I remembered the words that were spoken to me on my trip to Florida. This encouraged me so much because this was not an easy place to walk through, but I had no choice—it had to be done. I knew the challenge that lay before me, and I was reminded often by friends and family that God will never leave me.

Psalm 118:15-17 says, *"The voice of rejoicing and salvation is in the tents of the righteous…"* Now listen to this, *"The right hand of the Lord does valiantly, the right hand of the Lord is exalted, the right hand of the Lord does valiantly, I shall not die, but live, and declare the glory of the Lord."*

I knew I would live because I fully trusted in my wonderful Lord, believing in the mighty plans He had for the rest of my long life, or until His return.

5

GOOD NEWS

How beautiful upon the mountains are the feet of him who brings good news, who proclaims peace, who brings glad tidings of good things... (Isaiah 52:7).

Email to prayer intercessors and friends:

I can hardly believe that a week has flown by and all I've done is run to doctor appointments and have tests done. One of these was a colonoscopy, because cancer usually starts in places other than the lung.

Last Monday was the first appointment with Dr. Liu, my little "c" doctor—my oncology doctor. As I was leaving for my appointment, I received a call from Sue, our church intercessor. She called to pray for me, and I told her I had to leave for an appointment with my little "c" doctor. She asked me, "What is your little "c" doctor?" I said, "When I pray with cancer patients at a nearby hospital, I always say, 'Cancer is the little "c," but Christ is the big 'C.'" She laughed, and then prayed for me as I went out to get into my car.

When I met Dr. Liu, he was such a delight. All smiles and wonderful…I never had a doctor approach me with such a joyful spirit. He said to me, "You look so good!" I answered, "I feel good!" Then he said, "You are so positive," and I said, "I love the Lord." He said, "Oh, that's good!"

After all the questions and answers (my daughter Heidi was able to be with me through all my tests and doctor appointments), he told me that I would not need chemotherapy or radiation treatments. He said, "You'll be good with half a lung."

*After we finished, Heidi went back to work. I went to the bathroom at the doctor's office and started talking to the Lord. "I love You, Lord, and I know You can remove this little "c" spot, but I will be good with half of a lung." I started to laugh and started singing, "The joy of the Lord is my strength." God, You are so **faithful!***

...Do not sorrow, for the joy of the Lord is your strength (Nehemiah 8:10).

The results came back from my colonoscopy—my first since I was in my 20s—and the report was good and so they scheduled me for surgery.

I saw my surgeon, on Monday, February 21st, and I'm now scheduled for surgery on March 8th. I have first stage cancer in the upper right lung. They will remove the top part of my right lung, and I will be in the hospital from Tuesday through Wednesday. I really liked Dr. Kostin, he will do my surgery. He seems like such a caring doctor.

My daughter, who is a nurse living in California, will be coming next week to stay for two weeks. What a blessing to have two nurses in my family. My oldest granddaughter, Ashley, is a nurse practitioner and will stay with me for a week after Johanna has to go home. Sounds like a six to eight week time of recovery—but I'm praying for less. There are many friends signed up to come over and stay with me when they can—and even fix meals for me. I am so blessed!

I had a great surprise visit from my California friend, Mary. The Lord told her to fly out and spend a week with me. He said, "Mary, go out and stay with Donna." She paid her own way and flew to Pennsylvania! What a great visit we enjoyed and we praised God together for all His faithful servants He is sending to help me through this time. The Lord has given me a testimony in my life, and I believe even a stronger word to come forth.

Thank you for all your prayers.

Blessings,

Donna

6

MY MIGHTY ANGEL

Bless the Lord, you His angels, who excel in strength, who do His word, heeding the voice of His word (Psalm 103:20).

It was a couple of weeks before my surgery. I had called Richard Roberts' (Oral Roberts' Ministry) prayer line to pray for me. They sent me a small bottle of oil. I decided to take it to church and ask someone to pray for me. I had already had several of the pastors and their wives praying for me, but I decided to do it one more time. After the service, my friend Mary came to say hello and see how I was doing. I asked her, "Will you come up front with me and then let's see who the Lord will have pray over me today." So we went up to the front of the church and the Lord led me to Bob and Jeannie. I gave them the oil and Bob prayed first. He anointed my forehead and then my hands. He then gave the oil to his wife and she anointed the right side of my lung. I had never felt any pain in this area until she touched me. I was sure that I was healed at this time.

They prayed over me, and I was slain in the spirit and fell on the floor. While I was on the floor, the overwhelming presence of the Lord was all around me, and I said out loud, "Arise and shine oh daughter of Zion!" I started to laugh, because I thought of my precious husband who has been gone from my life for many years and is with Jesus. Early in the morning he would run into our bedroom and say, "Arise and shine oh daughter of Zion!"

As I sat up, Mary was holding me because I was so filled with the Holy Spirit I couldn't move. Then there was this cute little blonde boy about three years of age standing nearby staring at me. As I'm looking at him, Mary said, "Donna, he's looking right through you. Do you see how he's staring at you?" I said, "Yes, I guess I do."

I said to the little boy, "Can I give you a hug?" He ran over and gave me a big hug. Then he stepped back away from me and instead of looking in my eyes like he had before, he looked over my head and stared.

I said, "Do you see an angel?"

He said, "Uh huh."

"Is he my angel?"

He said, "Uh huh."

"Is he a mighty angel?"

He said, "Uh huh."

"Is he wearing purple?"

He said, "Uh huh."

And all I could say was, "WOW!" as the little boy turned around and ran off to play, forgetting totally about me.

Dressed in Purple

Now I can tell you how I know what my angel looks like. Several years ago when I was at a conference at Christ Community Church, the presence of the Lord had overwhelmed me. I was actually on the floor just praising the Lord. And somebody came up to me and said, "Do you know your angel is behind you?" I said, "Oh wow, I can feel the presence of the Lord all around me," but I didn't know my angel was behind me.

Then I saw our pastor's son, Brandon, and I looked at him because I know he sees angels. I motioned for him to come over to me and I asked him, "Can you see my angel?" As he stood quietly for a moment, he said, "Yes, I can. He's a warrior, and he's a mighty angel, and he is wearing purple."

"Wow, that is so cool," I said. "I know purple is royal, but my Lord, what does that mean?" Then a thought struck me, *You've called me to be a prayer intercessor since 1987, and now I understand how much I need that mighty warrior angel around me.*

Traveling with Angels

So now when I travel and when I get into my car, I thank the Lord for my angel before me, behind me, on top, underneath, and all around me in Jesus' name. A small side story: a friend of mine whose husband died and was having a tough time adjusting to the loss—this was before my husband died—came to stay with us for a couple of weeks. I would get in the car and say, "Thank You for my angel before me, behind me, on top, underneath, and all around me in Jesus' name." One day when we were returning home from running errands—(at this time she didn't know Jesus and later I had the blessing of leading her to the Lord)—she said, "Donna, do you realize there are no cars close in front of you and no cars close behind you?" I said, "Yes, I've noticed that at different times." I thought, *God how awesome You are that we can thank You for the protection around us.*

I can't help but think that we don't ask enough—and that's why we don't have enough.

…Yet you do not have because you do not ask (James 4:2).

I encourage you to ask for the presence of the Lord to be about you. Ask that the only words you speak today are words that God would use to edify the people around you. That's my heart. (I share more on this later because that's what God gave me for *The Circle of Prayer Ministry*.) It's what I pray every day as I anoint my head for His wisdom, His thoughts, His plans; my lips to speak only His word; my hands to be His vessels to do the work and plans that He has for us. Like His mighty angels who hear what He says and do only what He has called them to do.

7

OUT OF THE FIRE

...For He Himself has said, "I will never leave you nor forsake you" (Hebrews 13:5).

It was time to write to my prayer friends—it's only been a couple of weeks since surgery—time to give everyone an update. It was time to give the Lord thanks and praise for what He had brought me through.

Dear friends and family in Christ,

Before I share what has happened during these past weeks, I am reminded of how I traveled in the late '80s and early '90s with Rachel, the mother of Pastor Titus who was the pastor at that time of Christ Community Church. She was an evangelist, and I was so blessed to travel with her. We would go on short trips together and my husband would always say, "Donna, go!" because of the blessing she always was in my life. We became close friends. One thing this sweet evangelist friend of mine would often say to me was, "God doesn't make bridges, but He always walks you through whatever is put in front of you." And this I realized when I walked through the fire of cancer.

The day I went to the hospital seemed to be going okay. I was checked in for surgery. Just before I was going for anesthesia, I was blessed that Pastor Dave and Pastor Tim came and prayed for me. Some things I don't remember from that day, but I distinctly remember Pastor Dave saying, "Donna, I see your angel standing by you on your right side." Again—always on my right side—thank You, Lord, for the signs You give to me. I don't remember much about the surgery itself, I just went through it in peace. I had no anxiety about the fact that I was going to have half of my lung removed leaving a 14 inch scar on my body.

*My surgery on March 8th went very well. Dr. Kostin said that the cancer spot was the size of my thumb, under the 2 centimeter size. When he said this to me after the surgery I thought, **That's a small cancer—cancer is a small "c."** I think I questioned, "Why did I have that whole upper part of the lung removed?" My doctor said, "I got everything out that may have been cancerous." So as much as I really didn't want to lose a half of lung, my oncologist doctor had said, "You'll be good with half a lung!"*

A Revelation

During the recovery time I believe the Lord gave me a revelation about emotional and physical pain. The physical pain was so severe that it was hard to deal with anyone elses emotions. Zachery, my grandson who was 6 years old, asked his mommy, "Why is NaNa so sick that you have to go and stay with her so long?" Johanna flew in from California never having left her 2 children before in their life. He couldn't understand. Also, While she was with me, Zachery broke his arm and Katie was very sick—I remember the anguish of what she was feeling, but I was in such pain I had a hard time relating to her, even though I love my daughter and all my grandchildren very much.

*I thought, **Jesus took on every disease—everything upon Himself as He hung on the cross.** We can only feel a small iota of how excruciating His pain must have been. I know how my pain felt, and I know that His pain was beyond any of my understanding—this is what I understood as a revelation from God. I thought, **Jesus, You hung on the cross, You took on every disease, Your stripes were many—thirty-nine stripes on Your back—for every disease we could have. I only have one 14-inch stripe and I know how this feels and I know it's a revelation You want me to share.** As He hung on the cross, He looked down on those who were crucifying Him—who had made Him suffer—and said, "Father forgive them." Even in that time of excruciating pain that we can't even begin to imagine, He loved. He loved.*

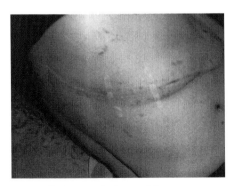

My fourteen inch one-stripe scar.

Sometimes it's hard to love when you're suffering and hurting and in excruciating pain—and I experienced this with the Lord. I think people need to know more of the fullness of what He did for us on the cross. And of course, we need to remember that He rose again and lives today! And we have the promise of eternity with Him. Hallelujah!

Isaiah 53:4-6 says:

Surely He has borne our griefs and carried our sorrows; yet we esteemed Him stricken, smitten by God, and afflicted. But He was wounded for our transgressions, He was bruised for our iniquities; the chastisement for our peace was upon Him, and by His stripes we are healed. All we like sheep have gone astray; we have turned, every one, to his own way; and the Lord has laid on Him the iniquity of us all.

People need to know that God has healing for our bodies. Even if we have to walk in pain or suffering, when we are His—when we give Him glory and praise and honor—He'll take us through whatever the pain is as long as we're praising Him and giving Him glory in the midst of whatever we're walking through.

The one thing that I know is that the prayers of family and friends are so important. It's hard to put that understanding into words. I know prayer with love carries us through.

After a week in the hospital, I went home. It has been wonderful having my daughters and grandchildren around me. I thank God daily for my family's love and help. My daughter Johanna stayed for two weeks with me; and my granddaughter Ashley stayed for a week caring for me. What a great blessing they were to me. Heidi and her husband, Joey, came as well as Joshua, and my oldest daughter, Luanne, and her daughter Brianna. What a blessing it was to me for those who could come.

The following week I was blessed with friends coming and staying overnight and fixing meals for me so I was never alone those first six weeks of recovery. Doctor Kostin said six to eight weeks of recovery; and in eight months I wouldn't even know that the right half of my lung is missing. I can say now I don't really miss it, but of course I would really love to have the Lord replace it—what an awesome glory to Jesus that would be! I can still hear my oncologist say, "You'll be good with a half lung."

*I'm walking in joy and peace knowing that the Lord cares and loves us in everything that He does. I keep thinking about the Scripture that the Lord gave to me in Florida: Jeremiah 33:3, **"Call to Me, and I will answer you, and show you great and mighty things, which you do not know."***

I'm walking in His joy and peace knowing that the Lord cares and loves us in everything that we do, and He has us in His hands. Please pray for my body to heal and pain to be gone as I walk through these next few months.

My heart is to glorify Jesus to everyone and in everything I do.

When you go through the fire and come out not smelling of smoke and without being burned, you know the glory of the Lord is with you.

Love in Christ,

Donna

8

THE BREATH
OF THE LORD

*The Spirit of God has made me, and
the breath of the Almighty gives me
life* (Job 33:4).

Email to family and friends:

*I've had several people ask how I was doing,
so here is an update. It has now been eleven
weeks since surgery, and wow, what an incredible time this has been. "God, You have been
with me in every area...in my tears, my joy and
laughter. So many wonderful revelations from*

You, Lord. I just hope I can put into words all that You've shown me."

When I was in the hospital for that first week, I was blessed to have my two nurse daughters, grandson, and son-in-law with me. Heidi would say, "Mom, you need to breathe deeper." With the pain I was in, I didn't want to hear that. What was interesting is that I had a little prayer book from Mary, my friend in California. I had been reading from it for my daily devotion, so I said, "Let me read this to you." I had just read the message "God's Power for Healing" about how faith gives substance to hope. As I finished reading the passage from this book out loud to everyone in the room, Heidi said, "Mom, do you realize how deep you were breathing as you read that to us?" I thought that was very interesting because I hadn't realized how deeply I was breathing. Then I was reminded that every word out of our mouth is from our heart.

> *For as he thinks in his heart, so is he…*
> *(Proverbs 23:7).*

Soon I was up out of bed and taking my little IV pole into the bathroom. Turning on the fan so no one could hear me, I started saying the Lord's Prayer—sometimes singing it and sometimes saying it:

> *Our Father in heaven, hallowed be Your name. Your kingdom come. Your will be done on earth as it is in heaven. Give us this day our daily bread. And forgive us our debts, as we forgive our debtors. And do not lead us into temptation, but deliver us from the evil one. For Yours is the kingdom and the power and the glory forever. Amen (Matthew 6:9-13).*

They told me I had to walk up and down steps before I could go home, because I have steps at my house. So I said, "Okay, I can do that." I had this one particular nurse with me; she's a nurse who speaks to people about their breathing after surgery and about getting stronger in breath. So as I was walking up the small steps, I turned to her and started to laugh and asked her, "Now what do I do that I'm up here?" She said, "You walk down." So I walked down the steps. It felt so good to laugh.

As we were walking up and down the hallway, I shared with her about reading the devotion and how my breathing had gotten deeper while I read it. I told her it might be something she could use with other patients about deep breathing. I said, "The breath of the Lord is life, and as you breathe deeply and speak deep words, your breath becomes stronger." I told her what I had read to my family and what my daughter Heidi had said about my breathing deeper. So I said, "Maybe you should have some of your patients read something to you and see how deeply they begin to breathe." I don't know if she did or not, but I thought it was a pretty good idea.

Thank you all for your prayers and for the thoughtful cards and emails, they mean so much.

Love and blessings in Christ,

Donna

****

After returning home and recuperating for more than five weeks, I decided to send out another email letting friends and family know of my progress.

Dear loved ones,

As some of you know I'm not a person to take drugs—I'm a nutritional girl—so as soon as I was able to, I stopped taking the narcotic drug at night that helped me sleep. The second night after I stopped taking the pain medicine, I woke up several times. I went back to bed, but I couldn't get back to sleep. So I decided to put some music on. I walked into my hallway and turned on a Christian station. The music was very soft. I went back to bed to listen to it. As I lay down on my bed, suddenly there were birds chirping at my window—I couldn't believe it! The noise was so loud it sounded as if they were in my room. I could hardly believe what I was hearing. The only tree I have near my house is in front of the bathroom that is at least 10 feet from my bed. As I'm lying there listening to the radio and the birds chirping, a song came on the radio and I began to sing along, "Holy, Holy, Holy, Lord God Almighty early in the morning my praise will rise to thee."

And as I sang that song, I realized the birds weren't chirping anymore. I lay there with an overwhelming peace and strength throughout me and thought, **Oh Lord, even the birds praise You in the morning; before we are even awake, they sing praises to You. They know You as Lord. You provide for them.** *I was reminded of the Scripture that says in Habakkuk 2:11 and Luke 19:40 that if we don't praise Him the rocks will cry out. How can I put into words what my heart was feeling for love and praise for the Lord at that moment?! The birds singing praises, the song, "Holy, Holy, Holy," and as I'm singing it I was filled with the breath and life of God. My whole being was immersed in His presence. I could not believe what was happening to my body.*

Miracle of Increased Breath

That same morning I received a call from a friend. First thing, 8:30 in the morning, I started sharing what I had experienced. And it seemed like I was talking to everybody that morning—sharing about how the breath of the Lord is life and how He spoke that to me—singing "Holy, Holy, Holy" to whomever would listen. After telling my story to several people I thought, **Here are these little birds with their little lungs praising You so loudly—I need to praise You with more strength in my voice.**

The last person I was singing the song to was my sister Lucille. When I got off the phone, I picked up my breathing apparatus; I was supposed to be able to reach 2,000 by blowing into it—I couldn't even get to 1,500! As I was sitting on the couch, I blew into it, and it read 2,000, then 2,500, 3,000, 3,500, 4,000, 4,500, and then 5,000! I said, "Wow, God! You are bringing my breath back to full capacity."

I heard the Lord say again to me, "The breath of the Lord is life." I thought, **Yes, Lord, You have given me life for the completion of Your destiny in my life.** *He keeps bringing me up to the third heaven where all we are to do is come into praise and glory for Him for what He has done in our lives.*

When I say I've walked through the fire and come through not smelling of smoke and not being burned, all I can do is sing praises to the glorious name of Jesus. God has brought me to such a place of knowing Him. I've known Jesus for many years. I rejoice when He says, **"He who is in you is greater than he who is in the world"** *(1 John 4:4). He said that to His disciples, He says it to us today.*

He sends the Holy Spirit—and that's a word I really want to get out. The Holy Spirit is here to speak to you, to show you ways to bring you to His fullness in your life. Lots of times when you don't know what you're doing, the Holy Spirit speaks to your heart and your ears, your mind, your soul, your being—what He wants you to know and where He wants you to walk. The truth is, I didn't want to go through this time with a little "c" cancer in my body, but the big "C" who is Christ held my hand and took me through many things in these past three months. Now eight months have gone by since my surgery. I saw Doctor Kostin and my report was good. He said, "I'll see you again in March when we'll do a yearly CT scan."

So again I'm at a point in my life where I say, "Thank You, Lord, for what You've done in my life. Thank You, Lord, for my children, my grandchildren, and my family; thank You for my pastor and for my friends from church;

thank You for my intercessors and all those you brought around me to draw us even closer to You."

*Mary, my California friend who stayed with me for a week—the one where the Lord told her, "Mary, go out and stay with Donna"—sent me a Scripture while she was in Thailand visiting her son and his wife who are missionaries there. She wrote, "Donna, you need to read the whole Scripture from Psalm 118." And when I looked at it, I laughed because it was in the middle of the whole chapter, but I had missed some of the Scripture when I was in Florida. I hadn't read the whole thing. Maybe it wasn't time to read those Scriptures through. But now I read Psalm 118:13, which says, **"You pushed me violently, that I might fall, but the Lord helped me."***

*I thought, **God is showing me everything that I walked through and the fullness of who He is and how He has helped me walk through it.** The Lord is my strength and my song, He is my salvation. What a wonderful confirmation of what I'd just walked through.*

I love you all and pray the Lord bless you and let His light shine upon you and His love surround you. Father has brought me to a place where I can rejoice in Jesus Christ even in the midst of the fire and the storms and the struggles.

Love,

Donna

My smile is totally due to His faithfulness and love

9

He Is Faithful

O LORD God of hosts, who is mighty like You, O LORD? Your faithfulness also surrounds You (Psalm 89:8).

Email to family and friends:

This is my year marker! Praise the Lord! "Can you believe that?" I said to friends at prayer training at Christ Community Church last night. Many said, "A year has gone by? Wow! I can hardly believe that." It has been quite a year of being closer to the Lord as never before in my life.

Today was my first year checkup with Doctor Kostin, and I was very happy with the report. He walked into the room and said that my CT scan was wonderful, no cancer, and the lung looked good. The right lung is as strong as the left lung, and my oxygen is level is 99 percent. I asked, "Did my right lung grow back yet?" He laughed and said, "No Donna, but it looks great." I had the opportunity to share even more of my testimony today with him. He said, "I'll see you in six months and we'll do another CT scan then." He gave me a hug and said, "I wish all my patients were like you, Donna."

Well, no creative miracle yet—but I must say what a mighty God we serve, and I am still believing that He will show Himself mighty in this area. He has been with me through this time of great trial. What the devil meant to destroy me, God has given me a mighty testimony to encourage others.

A friend said to me today, "Because you have overcome this cancer, you have the anointing and authority to pray for those who have cancer." As I like to say, cancer is the small "c" but Christ is the big "C."

So many words of strength were given to me by others, and I believe spoken directly from the heart of the Lord. As First John 4:4 says, **"He who is in you is greater than he who is in the world."** *If my heart can share one thought with you today it is, wherever you are walking or whatever you are walking through—whether it's a storm or a struggle—remember to fix your eyes only on Jesus. He is your everything.*

Psalm 118:8-17 (this has been a mighty word for my life) says:

> **It is better to trust in the Lord than to put confidence in man. It is better to trust in the Lord than to put confidence in princes. All nations surrounded me, but in the name of the Lord I will destroy them. They surrounded me, yes, they surrounded me; but in the name of the Lord I will destroy them. They surrounded me like bees; they were quenched like a fire of thorns; for in the name of the Lord I will destroy them. You pushed me violently, that I might fall, but the Lord helped me. The Lord is my strength and song, and He has become my salvation. The voice of rejoicing and salvation is in**

the tents of the righteous; the right hand of the Lord does valiantly. The right hand of the Lord is exalted; the right hand of the Lord does valiantly. I shall not die, but live, and declare the works of the Lord."

I want to thank everyone for your prayers for me and also the wonderful notes I received from you. Here are some, but not all of the encouraging words that were sent to me that have blessed my life:

Hi Donna, so happy to hear your good news! Am rejoicing with you. God is so good...Love and blessings to you.

Amen, Donna. You are a trophy of His grace, and all that you overcome is a testimony to all...The Father loves your faith and I pray for that creative miracle.

Praise God! We rejoice with you in this life giving gift from the Lord. You are a beautiful temple of the Holy Spirit.

Dear Donna, a great testimony and God is using you to reach others for Christ...

Rejoicing with you. He is faithful and mighty. Every blessing.

Rejoicing with those that are rejoicing! AMEN sister! I still believe that your creative miracle is already done in heaven and hasn't manifested on earth! In FAITH, God we stand in agreement!

Thank You, Lord, for all my brothers and sisters in faith who took the time to send such encouragement—I am so grateful.

I've given my life to Jesus and all I desire is to glorify Him. I pray the love of Christ draws you even closer to what He has for your life. As I close our time together, I'm excited about what the Lord will continue to show me. I pray He gives me His wisdom for the choices I have to make each day. I pray that what I have shared with you will make a difference in how you choose to walk through whatever is before you.

Again, I pray that God's rich blessings are with you and your loved ones.

Love in His name,

Donna

10

A Prophetic Word

And He Himself gave some to be apostles, some prophets, some evangelists, and some pastors and teachers, for the equipping of the saints for the work of ministry, for the edifying of the body of Christ (Ephesians 4:11-12).

I have attended several conferences and while the speakers pray for me, they have shared that the Lord will give me the creative miracle I've been asking for—for my lung to grow back. I've been asking the Lord to put that missing part of my lung back not because I'm not doing well, because

I am, but because I would love to share even more of what the Lord has done for me and can do in all of our lives.

Someone said to me, "You don't shut up now and I know when the Lord puts your lung back you'll never stop talking."

"Well," I said, "I plan to run around the world shouting what the Lord has done for me!" And with the publishing of this book, that is exactly what I plan to do—speaking wherever anyone would have me speak on how great and awesome our mighty God is.

A Prophetic Word

Recently a friend and I went to see Prophet John Mark Pool and his wife speak at a conference nearby. I've heard him speak before, but have never spoken to him personally. John Mark Pool and his wife had many prophetic words for those attending. It's interesting what I said to the Lord that night, "Lord, I want to hear a word from You tonight. Only a word from You." I wasn't thinking about what the word would be, only that the Lord would speak to me.

At the end of the conference I decided to buy one of John Mark's books. I was feeling finished with the event, but people were still being prophesied over. He was sitting at a table so I took the book over and asked him if he would sign it for me. He said, "Yes, what is your name?" I said, "Donna Beaver." He wrote in the book, then got up to go prophesy over someone. While I was sitting there waiting for my friend, I looked at my watch—it was 10:15. I thought to myself, *I'm tired, I think I'll just go home. You know what Lord, I really don't need a word from You tonight… You're enough for me.*

As I got up to leave, I saw that my friend was talking to John Mark. When I went over to say good night to her, he looked at me and asked, "What is your name again?" I said, "Donna Beaver." He looked at my friend and asked, "Who is Donna in the ministry?" She said, "She's a prayer coordinator." He looked at me and said, "Satan tried to kill you, but the Lord protected you because He has plans and destiny and purposes for your life." And then he said, "God has heard your heart cry for your children and your grandchildren, and He is going to bring them into the destiny, plans, and purposes He has for their lives."1 I just stood there and wept. I said, "God,

I asked for a word, but I had no idea of the word You would give me."

As I was driving home from the conference, I clearly heard the Lord speak to me, "It's time to finish the book." I have no doubt in my heart what He was saying to me.

Confirmation

John Mark's words of prophecy went right to my heart—that the Lord heard my prayer for my children and grandchildren and that He will bring them to the fullness of their destiny. That has been the cry of my heart to Him for so many years. Now, hearing with my own ears that He will bring them to their destiny—His plans and purposes for their lives—I was overcome. What an awesome God we serve. He is so faithful in His word. He is faithful in everything that we walk through.

The pushing of satan was real—he wanted to wipe out my life. I had no idea. I knew I was being pushed, I knew he was trying to steal the authority of Jesus in my life. But I had no idea that it was really to take my life. There was an attack from hell itself, but God was there all along—through the storms, in all my struggles, and in the midst of the fire of cancer.

ENDNOTE

1. I would like to add these words spoken by John Mark Pool: *"so that at the name of Jesus **every knee will bow**, of those who are in heaven and on earth and under the earth, and that every tongue will confess that Jesus Christ is Lord, to the glory of God the Father"* (Philippians 2:10-11 NASB). I wrote an e-mail to him asking if I could share the prophetic words he spoke over me and his response was: "Dear Donna: YES, by all means put my name in your book if you feel the Lord wants you to use it as a confirmation for your prophetic testimony for Gods glory! Thank you for asking and for sending this affirmation of testimony that encourages us as we travel and minister always praying the Word truly touches lives and transforms their setting to be God's person for their destiny." His ministry is: Word to the World Ministries; www.w2wmin.org.

II

The Reality of the Spiritual World

*For we do not wrestle against flesh and
blood, but against principalities, against
powers, against the rulers of the dark-
ness of this age, against spiritual hosts
of wickedness in the heavenly places*
(Ephesians 6:12).

Are Angels Real?

After reading my testimony, you've got to believe
in angels—from the oil on my eye glass lens, to the
little boy awestruck by what he saw, to my pastor seeing one standing by my right side before surgery.

Yes, I believe in angels.

I've asked people, "Do you believe in angels?" And most people do believe in angels. And I've asked people, "Do you believe angels are here on earth around us, or are they just in Heaven?" People have replied to me, "Yes, I believe angels are around us." But people have also responded, "Well, they're kind of in Heaven." The Scriptures say that God sends our angels to take care of us, to protect us here on earth:

For He shall give His Angels charge over you, to keep you in all your ways (Psalm 91:11).

And that they are in Heaven too:

All the angels stood around the throne and the elders and the four living creatures, and fell on their faces before the throne and worshiped God... (Revelation 7:11).

Is Jesus Real?

I've heard bold witnesses from people from other countries who have seen angels, and also others who have been protected by angels in mighty ways. And so when I've asked people, "Do you believe in angels?" and they say, "Yes! They are very real," my next question to them has been, "Well if you believe in angels, do you believe how real Jesus Christ is?" And most people say, "Yes I believe Jesus Christ is real." And then I ask, "Have you accepted Him as Lord and Savior of your life?" And then the perfect follow-up is to ask, "Would you like to accept Jesus as Lord and Savior of your life right now?"

> *Therefore God also has highly exalted Him and given Him the name which is above every name, that at the name of Jesus every knee should bow, of those in heaven, and of those on earth, and of those under the earth, and that every tongue should confess that Jesus Christ is Lord, to the glory of God the Father* (Philippians 2:9-11).

Is Satan Real?

And then, what about satan? Do we think he's a little hidden thing? Well, he is under our feet—the word of God says that:

> *Behold, I give you the authority to trample on serpents and scorpions, and over all the power of the enemy, and nothing shall by any means hurt you.* (Luke 10:19)

We also know from Scripture that satan comes to rob steal and destroy. The word of God says:

The thief [satan] does not come except to steal, and to kill, and to destroy. I [Jesus] have come that they may have life, and that they may have it more abundantly (John 10:10).

And he dwells here on earth:

So the great dragon was cast out, that serpent of old, called the Devil and Satan, who deceives the whole world; he was cast to the earth, and his angels were cast out with him (Revelation 12:9).

The Spiritual World Is Real

When I share the testimony about what I've walked through, there is no denying how real and awesome Jesus and His angels are and how real but insignificant satan is. I think of the words that I heard from the prophetic speaker—who had to ask me twice "Who are you?"—yet the Lord spoke mightily through him that night. "Yes, satan tried to kill you, but I was there protecting you, because I have plans and destiny and purpose for you." And then my heart was truly blessed because I prayed for years for my children and grandchildren. God heard my heart cry, and He said, "I will bring them all to the destiny, plans, and purposes that I have for each one of their lives." Now I had heard someone speak it who had no idea of what I had gone through. Jesus is my Source, my Strength, my Lord and Master, my Husband—He is everything to me.

Lord, always keep me walking in Your righteousness and love.

Words of Encouragement

If you have not made the commitment to except Jesus into your heart, I pray that you take the time and do it now. Read John 3:16: *"For God so loved the world that He gave His only begotten Son, that whoever believes in Him should not perish, but have everlasting life."*

All you have to do is know you are a sinner and need to be saved by grace. Believe that Jesus loves you so much that He died for you. Believe that He rose again and He sent the Holy Spirit to teach you.

However, when He, the Spirit of truth, has come, He will guide you into all truth; for He will not speak on His own authority, but whatever He hears He will speak; and He will tell you things to come (John 16:13).

Become the person God wants you to be. See yourself coming into your destiny. Believe—faith believes it will happen, when it has not yet come. Let your faith arise because God is *faithful! faithful!* FAITHFUL!

Ask Jesus. Ask Jesus—I don't think we ask the Lord enough. Ask Him: What are You saying to me? What are You doing in my life? What do You want me to do for You? As I look back on my life, there have been many times I've asked the Lord these questions and I can tell you He is *faithful!* Jesus tells us to ask of Him—so ask! I also know of the many times He has shown me things and spoken words to me. He tells us many things, unfortunately many times we don't listen to what He is saying or we don't want to hear it. Keep your heart soft to hear the voice of His Spirit.

> *So I say to you, ask, and it will be given to you; seek, and you will find; knock, and it will be opened to you* (Luke 11:9).

Pray and ask Jesus, "If You are alive, then show me that I might know You and serve You. I want to know the truth, for the truth will set me free."

> *Then Jesus said to those Jews who believed Him, "If you abide in My word, you are My disciples indeed"* (John 8:31).

I hope that my sharing will open the door for you to a new relationship with Jesus.

I pray the power of the Holy Spirit rests upon you and gives you His peace.

12

The Circle of Prayer

Finally, my brethren, be strong in the Lord and in the power of His might (Ephesians 6:10).

I'm sure you may have walked through storms in your life and had to work through a struggle or two. God doesn't say we won't have times of trial, but His word does say He will never leave us or forsake us.

*Let your conduct be without covetousness; be content with such things as you have. For He Himself has said, **"I will never leave you nor*** *forsake you." So we may boldly say: "The Lord is my helper; I will not fear. What can man do to me?* (Hebrews 13:5-6)

Old Is Past, New Is Yet to Come

Throughout the book I mentioned The Circle of Prayer, which has influenced my walk with the Lord and my faith tremendously. The history of its beginning started in 2002 when I attended a Sunday night service at a local Church in Hershey, Pennsylvania. Pastor Phil Cappuccio had a prophetic word over me that night that prompted stirrings in me that would eventually give birth to *The Circle of Prayer* ministry.

The pastor's words to me follow:

Through your life; you'll break open the bread of life. (Where did that come from?) You'll speak out of the resources I have put in you. Change your mindset as who you know yourself to be. I call you minister, ambassador. Keep your Bible and notebook open in the night prayer. Think you are not a slow learner. Don't limit Me; I can do anything I desire. Keep your sword sharp and by your side. You will bring the word of the Lord. You shall be one of the sons and daughters in the prophetic word. Many assignments I'll

*send you prepared—a new boldness is coming.
Old is past, new is yet to come. You are My
handmaiden.*

It seems strange how we sometimes hear a word
and put it aside instead of obeying the Lord—I have
done this myself on occasion. This time I listened,
and I put my Bible, notebook, and pen by my bed-
side. I had no idea how the Lord would begin to
have me write notes in the early hours. I had been
a prayer intercessor for many years before this, but
I still asked the Lord frequently how I should begin
praying and spending time with Him. I came upon a
small pamphlet called ACTS (unfortunately I cannot
find it to this day or I would reference it for you). I
started reading it and loved the layout of "Beginning
Your Prayer time with Jesus." It presented a plan of
praying: A-Adoration, C-Confession, T-Thanksgiv-
ing, S-Supplications. So I began my prayer times by
using this format.

Time passed after receiving the prophetic word,
and I made plans to visit my daughter, Johanna, in
California, as I try to do several times a year. My
friend Mary asked me if I would like to hear Beni
Johnson (intercessor and senior pastor, along with
her husband, Bill Johnson, of Bethel Church) speak
at Harvest Christian Center in Turlock, a few miles
from Modesto. What an awesome day of teaching

it was. It was the first time I had experienced soaking with music and spending time hearing and loving the Lord. There we were lying on the church pews just soaking in the presence of the Lord—this was an encounter that profoundly affected me.

Steps to Follow

It was a short time after coming back from this trip that the Lord woke me up at 4:30 in the morning. I sat up in bed hearing what the Lord was setting before me. And guess what—I had my Bible, notebook, and pen beside me, and I started writing. From this time spent with Him I wrote down the steps to follow for The Circle of Prayer—coming together for a time of unity prayer and making it a day of fasting and praying together the words that spell out A.C.T.S.

He reminded me of the Trinity and three being complete—Father, Son, and Holy Spirit.

Though one may be overpowered by another, two can withstand him. And a threefold cord is not quickly broken (Ecclesiastes 4:12).

The Lord also told me, "Come together every week or once a month and plan this day to be a Celebration Fast." I encourage you to plan a Celebration

Fast and to fast when you meet with your prayer partners. There are many kinds of fasts. Here are some suggestions, but do as the Lord leads you:

1. Liquid fast – No food only liquid.

2. Daniel fast – Daniel 1:12: *"Please test your servants for ten days, and let them give us **vegetables** to eat and **water** to drink."*

3. Choose your own fast as the Lord leads.

Remember, you come together for the purposes of God. In Matthew 9:15, our Lord said His disciples will fast. He shared that fasting is a personal matter between you and God and to be beautiful in your fast to the Holy One so no one will look at you as if you are pious or godly.

But you, when you fast, anoint your head and wash your face, so that you do not appear to men to be fasting, but to your Father who is in the secret place; and your Father who sees in secret will reward you openly (Matthew 6:17-18).

After fasting and coming together in your group of two, three or more, join hands and pray the Lord's Prayer:

Our Father in heaven, hallowed be Your name. Your kingdom come. Your will be done on earth as it is in heaven. Give us this day our daily bread. And forgive us our debts, as we forgive our debtors. And do not lead us into temptation, but deliver us from the evil one. For Yours is the kingdom and the power and the glory forever. Amen (Matthew 6:9-13).

There are supplies you will need for the next part of your time together. They are: Bridal Intercession Oil (or any oil that's been prayed over will do), bread and wine for communion, and a notepad and pen.

The next thing to do is pray ACTS:

- Adoration: Adoration of the Lord. Praise Him. Love Him. Honor Him.

- Anointing: (the Lord had me add this) Take the oil and anoint your mind for His wisdom—

  Let this mind be in you which was also in Christ Jesus...(Philippians 2:5)

  your mouth for speaking the words that He gives to you—

Let the words of my mouth and the meditation of my heart be acceptable in Your sight, O Lord, my strength and my Redeemer. (Psalm 19:4)

and your hands for healing and doing the work of the Lord.—

Lift up your hands in the sanctuary, and bless the Lord. (Psalm 134:2)

- Confession: What you see as your short-comings in your life, confess.

- Communion: (the Lord also had me add this) After confessing your sins, take communion, which is the Covenant that God gave to us to remember that Christ died for us.

- Thanksgiving: After communion, give thanks to God for who He is in your life.

- Supplication: Ask the Lord for your prayer needs and ministry requests.

- Soaking: (the Lord had me add this as well) As you lay quietly, begin to fix your eyes on Jesus and tell Him how much you love Him. I have found it is better to play music with no words for 15 to 20 minutes. This is a time to have your pen and note-book ready to write down whatever you hear from the Lord.

When you finish your time together, you may share what the Lord has said to you, unless it is too personal.

Since writing The Circle of Prayer—and praying this way for several years—I believe that this is a time of preparation for the Bride of Christ.

The Right Hand and Left Hand

In August 2011 I was teaching a class on The Circle of Prayer. This was a setup for a state prayer coordinator in the State College area of Pennsylva-nia. She had invited her team of prayer intercessors, and they had gathered together and were sitting in a circle. I like to bring people together in a circle for unity. When we were sitting in a circle, I prayed for the person sitting on the right and we went around praying for each other. Not one person praying for everybody, but each praying for the person next to them on the right. I talked about the authority of Jesus Christ being in our right hand. Then someone asked, "What's in our left hand?" I started laughing and said, "I don't know, but I'll pray about it and get back to you."

We had a wonderful time praying for each other that evening; but when we were finished, the question the woman had asked me was still on my mind as I drove home that night.

I had prayer the next morning with three other women. We were sitting in a circle as we always do, then out of the blue I started laughing. I just love when the Lord speaks to my heart and I hear Him say something to me. I started sharing with these women about the right hand being the authority of Jesus Christ in our life. Than suddenly I started hearing from the Lord about the left hand. He said, "The left hand represents the Holy Spirit!" I stood there with my arms stretched out, and I started to weep— because, "It's all about Jesus hanging on the cross dying for us and bringing salvation to our lives for the promise of eternity."

Holding up my right hand I said, "Here's the authority," then holding up my left hand I said, "Here's the power." He showed me that when we grab hands in a circle, we're grabbing the authority of Jesus Christ in our right hand and the person on our right is grabbing the power of the Holy Spirit in their hand. And what we take hold of is His authority and power! That's why I believe the circle and holding hands is so powerful.

I was questioning within myself, *"Is my revelation about the hands written in the word of God?"* during this time I was planning to go to California. I'm always blessed to have the opportunity to pray with Pastor Rick Countryman, my California pastor. When we got together, I was sharing with him what God had shown me about our right and left hands symbolizing the authority of Jesus and the power of the Holy Spirit. My question to him, "Is it written in the word about the power of the Holy Spirit in our left hand or left side?" His reply, "No, I can't say it is. But what a beautiful revelation you've received from the Lord. Don't let go of the fullness of what the Lord is saying in this revelation. God shows us many powerful things about who He is."

> *The secret things belong to the LORD our God, but those things which are revealed belong to us and to our children forever, that we may do all the words of this law* (Deuteronomy 29:29).

The Kingdom is a seed that must be sowed. Renew you mind daily with the word of God. Remember, what you focus on you will become. God has mighty plans for His end-time Bride. I pray this outline is truly a blessing and a guide for all that the

Lord has for the days ahead. May He truly impart His heart every time you come together in your Circle of Prayer.

I close this chapter of my book with the words of our Father God knowing that prayer is the authority that unlocks the key to the Kingdom of God.

But seek first the kingdom of God and His righteousness, and all these things shall be added to you (Matthew 6:33).

DONNA BEAVER

I live in Hummelstown, Pennsylvania—about two miles from Hershey Park, if you enjoy chocolate or are a fan of amusement park rides. My deceased husband, Frank, loved Hershey Park, and when I moved here I asked the Lord, "Why here? Why Hershey?" Frank's the one who loved Hershey but over time I have come to love it too.

I was born in Jamestown, New York, the youngest of four girls. My parents were from Sweden, so I'm the first generation born in America. I grew up in Falconer, New York, and after we married we moved to Hornell, New York. We lived in our funeral home in Hornell, where we raised our girls.

We moved to Lewisberry, Pennsylvania, to buy a funeral home in 1984, it was a move of the Lord, but that's another story...

I'm a member of Christ Community Church in Camp Hill, Pennsylvania, and have been there for twenty-eight years. Dave Hess is the pastor, and I'm very blessed to be in the body of Christ at this church.

I have three beautiful, married daughters and have been blessed with seven grandchildren—five granddaughters and two grandsons.

My heart cry as you read my book (which is my testimony of the greatness of Christ in my life) is that you will come into a personal relationship with Jesus—and if you already know Him, that you will be drawn even deeper and closer to Him. The miracles shared throughout this book—the Lord sending people to me I had not seen in years to pray for me; people I didn't know giving me words from the Father to encourage me; the wonderful gift of knowing my angel was protecting me; and many more, point to a personal and loving Savior who is undeniable.

I pray that you will come into the fullness of Jesus in your life and the power of His Holy Spirit. May you hear Him speaking to you today directing your steps toward your God-given destiny!

There is no greater way than the way of the Lord. He is our everlasting peace.

If you would like me to share my testimony with your women's ministry, church, cancer group, or conference about what God has brought me through, please email me at: stormsandfire@google.com.

Or you can write to:

Donna Beaver
PO Box 155
Hummelstown, PA 17036

In His precious love,

Donna Beaver

NOTES

NOTES

NOTES

NOTES

NOTES

NOTES

NOTES

NOTES